OPTOMETRIST

© 2024 Julie Dascoli

All rights reserved. No part of this book may be reproduced or transmitted in any form or by any means, electronic or mechanical, including photocopying, recording or by any information storage and retrieval system, without prior permission in writing from the publisher.

Published in 2024 by Amba Press, Melbourne, Australia.
www.ambapress.com.au

Previously published in 2015 by Hawker Brownlow Education.
This edition replaces all previous editions.

ISBN: 9781923116863 (pbk)
ISBN: 9781923116870 (ebk)

A catalogue record for this book is available from the National Library of Australia.

Real People
Real Careers

OPTOMETRIST

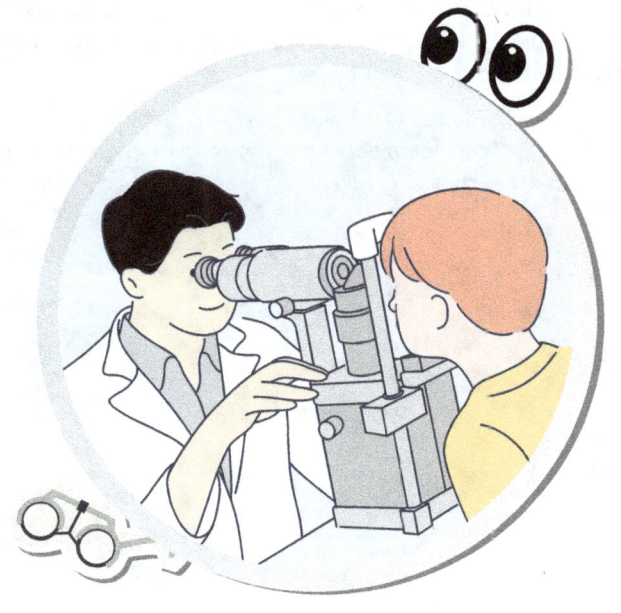

Written by Julie Dascoli

Photography by Laura Dascoli

Dear Reader,

Welcome to this volume of the *Real People Real Careers* series. I hope you'll enjoy learning all about Joe and his work as an optometrist.

Before you read on, I'd like to say a few thank-yous to the people who helped to make this book possible.

Firstly, thank you to Laura Dascoli, who took the photographs you see in the book, and to Donna Dascoli, who provided initial editing and computer support services.

Secondly, my thanks to the staff and students in Years 4, 5 and 6 of the Mossgiel Park Primary School class of 2015 for their unwavering help and support.

And finally, I'm grateful to Joe himself, who generously gave up his time to help others learn about his profession – and to show them all the ways in which his job rules!

Happy reading!

Julie Dascoli

OPTOMETRIST

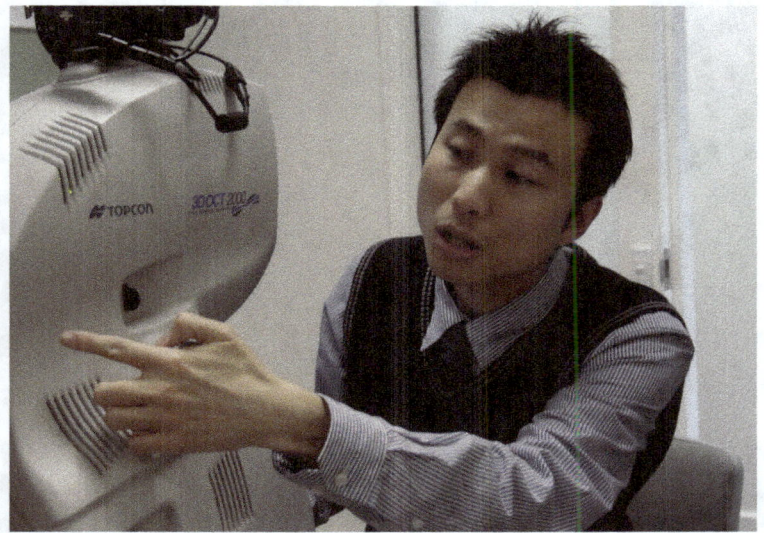

My name is Joe and I am an **optometrist**.

I completed primary school and the first two years of high school in Hong Kong, my country of origin. I **migrated** to Australia with my family and completed my remaining years of high school in Australia. The move was a big adventure for my family, but we soon got used to living in Australia.

Some of the subjects I took at my local high school were **chemistry**, **physics**, maths and English. I knew I wanted a career in the healthcare field, and I thought these subjects would keep my options open. English was a little challenging as it is my second language, although I did learn some English in Hong Kong. I just had to work a bit harder to master the language, and before long it was no problem at all.

In Year 12, I went to open days at a few **universities**. These events were very interesting, as we got the chance to tour the **faculties** that we were interested in and talk to **lecturers** and current students. I found this experience to be very helpful when the time came to decide what job I'd like to do.

After working hard and finishing high school, I obtained a place in an optometry course at a **renowned university**. I knew it was going to be a busy and challenging course, but I was ready and excited to get started.

During my first few years at **university**, I did subjects like **chemistry**, **physics**, **statistics** and a few optometry-related subjects. I attended **lectures** and **tutorials** and did plenty of study to absorb the information being taught so that I would know everything I could about eyes.

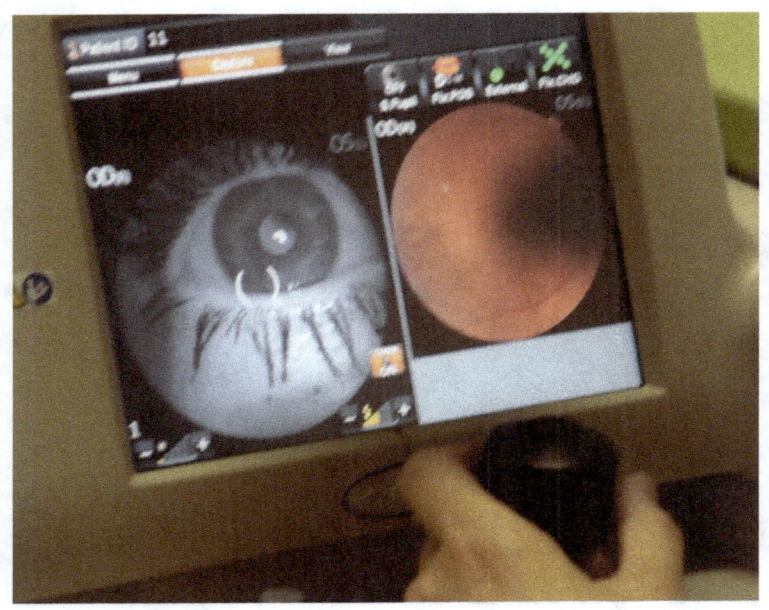

OPTOMETRIST

In my final year, I did **clinical training** at a working **clinic** set up at the college. In this setting, I was able to see patients and learn how to **consult** with them regarding their eye care needs. I had to **examine** their eyes under the supervision of a **qualified optometrist**, but I would do the complete consultation with the patient and the supervisor would only step in when required.

The optical field, like all other medical fields, is always **evolving**. There are always new types of **equipment**, new medicines and new **techniques** being developed, all of which are beneficial to patients now and in the future.

In order to stay current with all of these developments, **optometrists** are required to attend ongoing training in the form of **seminars**, **workshops** and **conferences**.

Optometrists are also required to be registered with **AHPRA**, which stands for the Australian Health Practitioner Regulation Agency. This is the governing body of optometry in Australia.

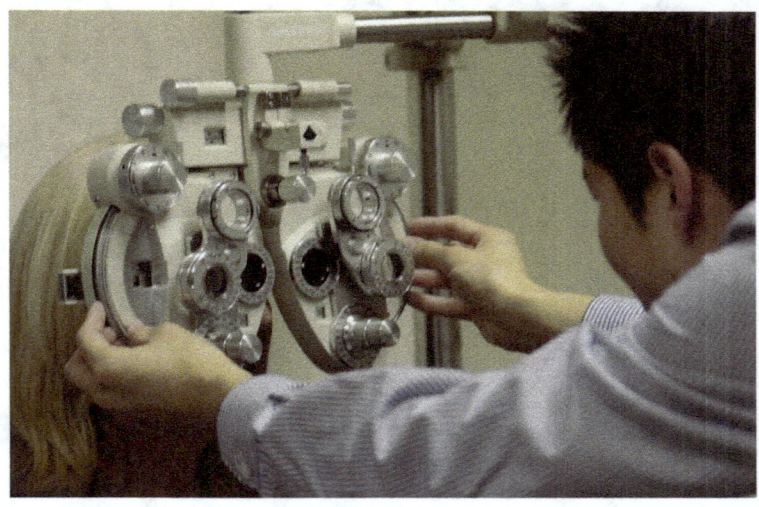

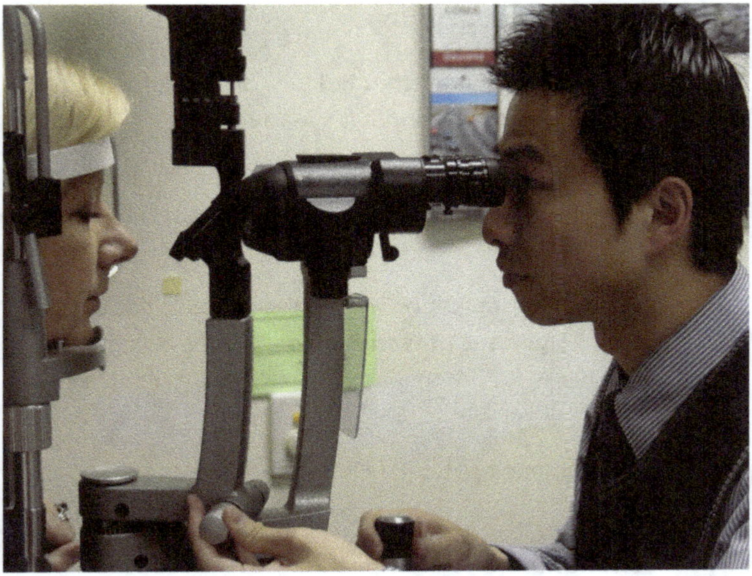

OPTOMETRIST PAGE 5

Tasks I perform every day

- On arrival at work each day, I turn on the lights and set up my **clinic** room so that it's ready for the day.

- I call in each patient one at a time in the order that they have been scheduled by the **receptionists**. I then begin consultation.

- I record information on a consultation card about the patient's **glasses prescription** or treatment, along with any other information that will help me with the patient's eye care.

- Between each patient, I fill in paperwork.

- Eventually I stop for lunch! Then, after lunch, I continue **consulting**.

- At the end of the day, I tidy the room, shut down the **equipment** and go home.

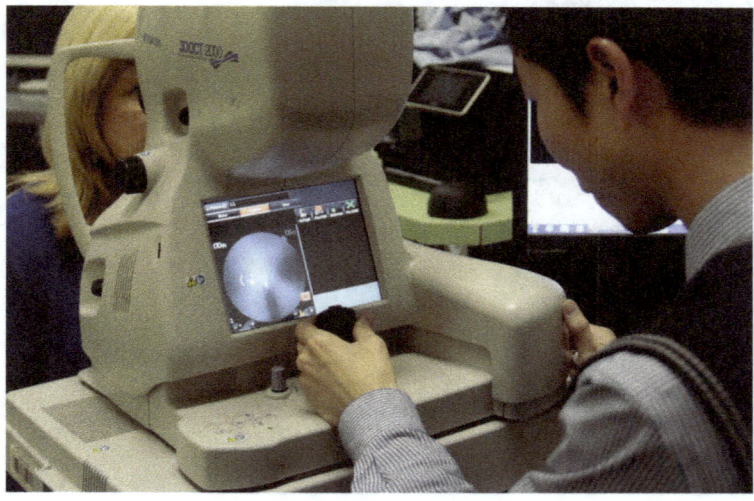

Interesting facts about my job

- I work eight-to-nine hours per day.
- My lunchbreak lasts for 45 minutes.
- I see 12–14 patients each day.
- My least favourite task is encountering eye problems that cannot be cured.
- My favourite task is teaching students and watching them develop.
- My dream job is what I am doing now.
- The college where I work has many **clinics** within it, including a contact lens **clinic**, a children's **clinic**, an ocular disease **clinic** and a disability **clinic**.

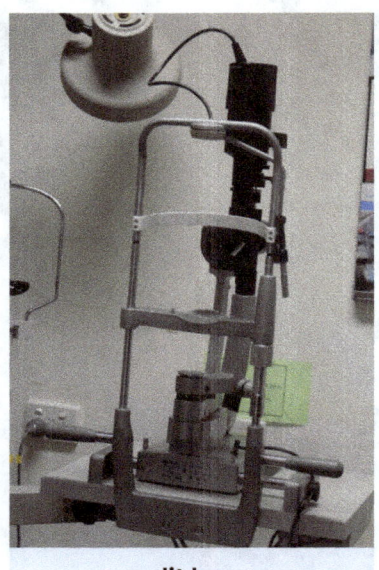

split lamp

I am trained to use a vast variety of tools and **equipment**. The one below is a corneal topographer, which is used for mapping the outer surface of the eye.

I must wash my hands thoroughly between patients, as **hygiene** is very important.

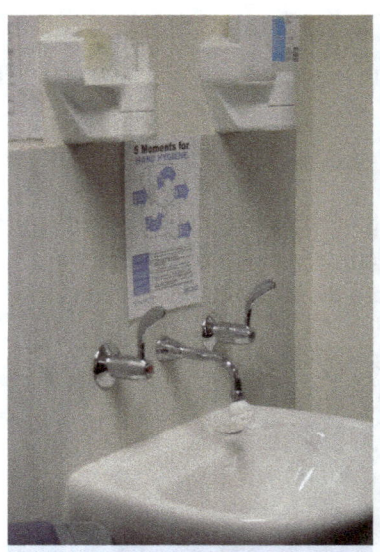

sink for handwashing

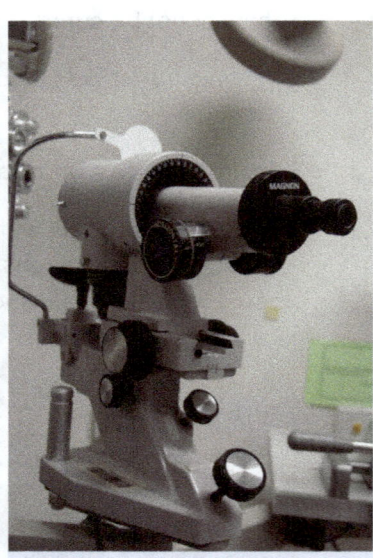

corneal topographer

The optical field, like all other medical fields, is always evolving. There are always new types of equipment, new medicines and new techniques being developed, all of which are beneficial to patients now and in the future.

What I wear to work

I must present myself in a professional way. This picture shows the way I dress for work each day. As an optometrist, wearing a clinic uniform enhances our professional image, fosters patient trust, and ensures a clean and organised environment.

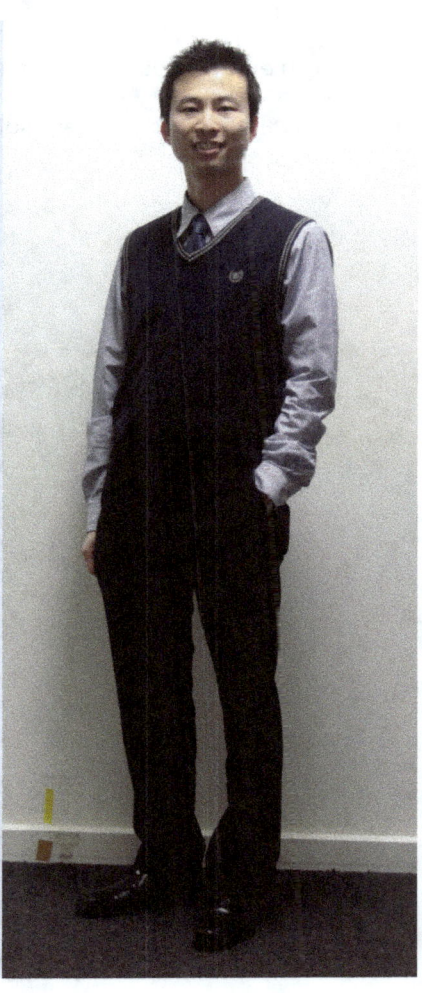

> As an optometrist, wearing a clinic uniform enhances our professional image, fosters patient trust, and ensures a clean and organised environment.

What you need to do this job

- → You are a caring person.
- → You like, or are good at, science subjects.
- → You enjoy talking to different kinds of people of varying ages.
- → You enjoying using equipment.
- → You are a good problem-solver.

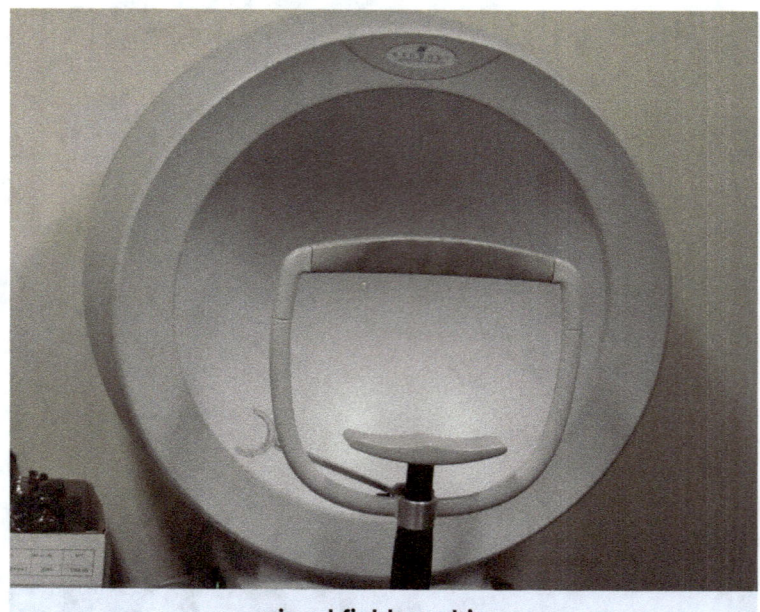

visual field machine

Related occupations

- paediatric **optometrist**
- ophthalmologist (to do this job, you would need to get a medical degree first and then specialise in eyes afterwards)
- research scientist
- contact **optometrist**
- **clinic receptionist**

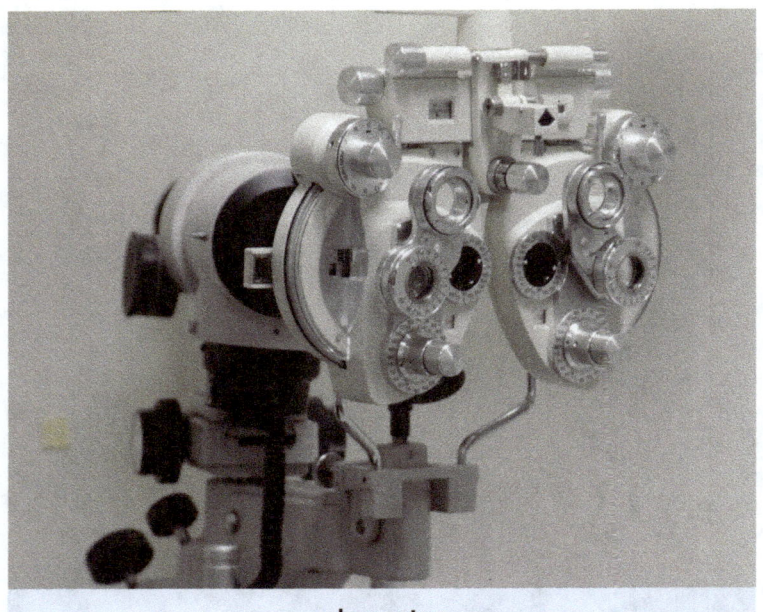

phoropter

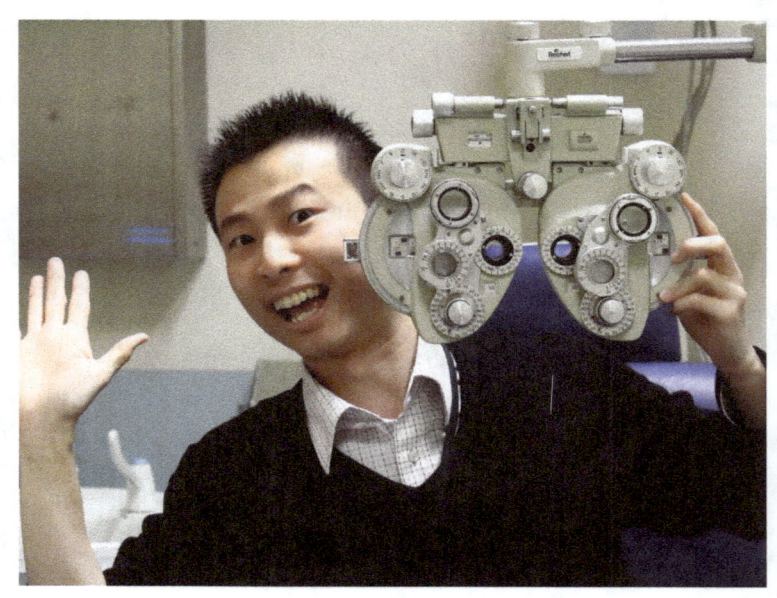

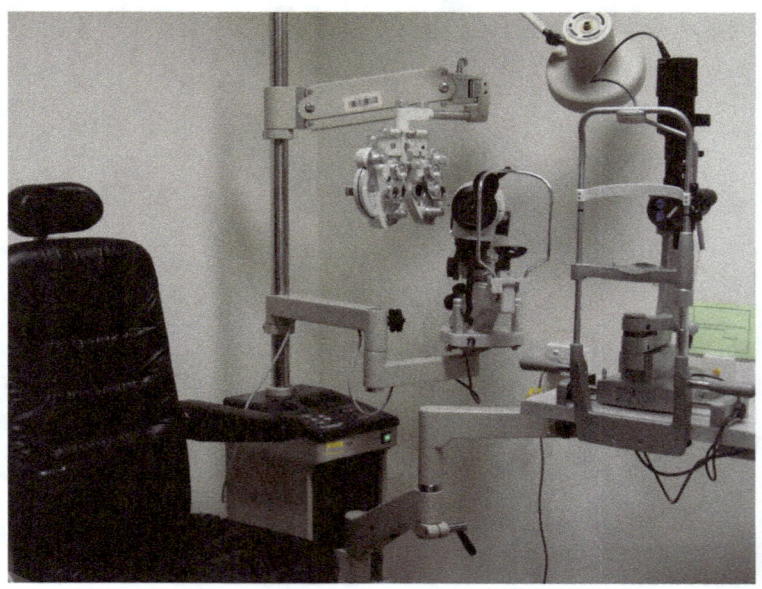

Postscript

Joe is now not only an **optometrist** but also a clinical teaching **coordinator**. He organises placements for students in the many different **clinics** within the college and supervises their progress.

This is Joe's dream job.

Glossary

AHPRA The Australian Health Practitioner Regulation Agency. This is the governing body of optometry in Australia. *It is compulsory for Joe to be a member of **AHPRA**.*

Chemistry The branch of physical science concerned with the composition, properties and reactions of substances. *Joe studied **chemistry** as a subject during high school and at **university**.*

Clinic The offices in which medical professionals like optometrists meet with and examine patients. *The college where Joe works has many **clinics** within it, including a contact lens **clinic**, a children's **clinic**, an ocular disease **clinic** and a disability **clinic**.*

Clinical training The training component of a course, in which students are supervised while practising on real patients. *Joe participated in **clinical training** during the last year of his course.*

Consult The act of treating patients and advising them of the best treatment for their eye care. *Joe **consults** with patients on a daily basis.*

Coordinator — Someone whose task is to make sure that a situation runs smoothly. *Joe has managed to get his dream job and is now a clinical teaching **coordinator**.*

Equipment — The tools that a person needs in order to do their job. *Joe uses a variety of **equipment** when he **examines** people's eyes to see if they might need a **glasses prescription**.*

Evolve — To develop and change gradually. *All medical fields **evolve**, meaning that new developments happen all the time.*

Examine — To inspect thoroughly – in this instance, to determine the condition of the eye. *When Joe **consults** with a patient, he **examines** their eyes.*

Faculty — A department in a **university** that specialises in a certain subject. *Joe was interested in the science **faculty**, as this is where students learn the skills required for health-related jobs.*

Glasses prescription — The lenses of glasses that have been made specifically to match the wearer's defects of vision. *Joe **examines** each patient's eyes to determine if they need a **glasses prescription**.*

Hygiene	Conditions and practices that serve to promote or preserve health. *Joe washes his hands between patients because **hygiene** is very important.*
Lecture	An educational talk to an audience, especially students at a **university**. *Joe learnt a lot when he attended **university lectures**.*
Lecturer	The people who conduct **lectures** at universities. They are the teachers in higher education. *Joe was able to talk to **lecturers** when he visited **university** open days.*
Migrate	To move from one place or country to another. *When Joe was a high school student, he **migrated** from Hong Kong to Australia with his family.*
Optometrist	The healthcare profession concerned with the examination, diagnosis and treatment of the eyes using lenses and other optical aids. *Once Joe finished **university**, he was a **qualified optometrist**.*

Physics   The science that deals with matter, energy, motion and force. *Joe studied **physics** as a subject during high school and at **university**.*

Qualified   When a student is shown to have obtained the necessary skills to do a job, usually after finishing a course, they are deemed to be **qualified**. *A **qualified optometrist** oversees optometry students during their **clinical training**.*

Receptionist   An office worker who answers phones, greets people when they enter the office and answers questions in order to assist clients. *At Joe's **clinic**, the **receptionist** makes appointments for the patients.*

Renowned   Having a good reputation or being famous. *Joe obtained a position to study optometry at a **renowned university**.*

Statistics   The branch of mathematics that deals with the collection, organisation, analysis and interpretation of numerical data. *Joe studied **statistics** as a subject at **university**.*

Technique   A method of doing a task or performing something. *New **techniques** are being developed in all fields of medicine.*

Tutorial   A lesson at **university** that is more casual and interactive than a **lecture**. Students can ask questions rather than just listen and take notes. *In addition to **lectures**, Joe also attended **tutorials** at **university**.*

University   A tertiary education facility where students can obtain a **qualification**. *Joe went to open days at many **universities** to try and work out what he wanted to do as a job.*

Other titles in this series

www.ingramcontent.com/pod-product-compliance
Lightning Source LLC
Chambersburg PA
CBHW070343120526
44590CB00017B/3000